THE VERDICT- THE WAY FORWARD FOR SPEECH CENSORSHIP AND INTERMEDIARIES

SANDHIYA K

Made with ❤ on the Notion Press Platform
www.notionpress.com

Contents

Preface

"Start writing, no matter what. The water does not flow until the faucet is turned on".

- Louis L'Amour

Hundreds of students and professors are contributing their work to Brillopedia, we are here to provide ample information about Law and Contemporary issues. Our aim is to provide a platform for today's generation to express their views and ideas on law and contemporary law.

Author

Sandhiya K

CHAPTER ONE

Abstract

Hate- a word to describe an emotion that has an intensive disliking towards a person or a thing. It can also take form of an unstated violence that could create harm, threat or injury to a person. In the cyber world, there is a wide scope for threatening, intimidating or offending a person which requires stringent regulations to protect the netizens. But what amounts to an offense or hate is a million dollar question to be answered. The major breakthrough in this tussle was the Shreya Singhal Case where Section 66A of the Information Technology Act was struck down by the Hon'ble Supreme Court of India. This law was even dubbed by many to be draconian due to the repercussions it has created. For a statement to be defamatory or injurious it is important to understand what is the reasonable interpretation of a statement being hazardous and the duty of the intermediary platform to the public. This paper is an attempt to understand the way forward post the removal of Section 66A and the responsibilities of an intermediary in the cyberspace.

CHAPTER TWO

Introduction

It has been seven years since the iconic Shreya Singhal v. Union of India judgement was passed. Since then, the question of free speech and hate speech; the liability of an intermediary and the impact of this verdict on the current internet servers and users have tremendously gained attention. Speech cannot be absolute and there has to be a line properly drawn to distinguish between what is hate speech and what is in violation of Article 19 (1) (a) of our Constitution. This paper is an attempt to elaborate and magnify this so-called *ghost section* and the liability of intermediaries and map out the way forward to guide the upcoming disruptions with regard to free speech.

When we analyse the reason why the Honourable Apex Bench decided to strike down Section 66-A of the Information Technology Act,2000, we can observe the Court's stance which explains that mere violation of an individual's sentiment cannot be a bar on the freedom of speech and expression. Such a limitation cannot be a backbone to legitimize Section 66-A. But this does not in any way promote absolute speech without any filters. For instance, the cut-off for the quoting and plea of offending religious sentiments under Section 295-A of IPC is lesser than that which is required for sedition.

CHAPTER THREE

Free Speech and Hate Speech – A Malleable Border

The question that needs to be answered is with regard to what would come under the ambit of free and absolute speech. The issue becomes more complex when there are certain statements written and expressed without any malicious intention but would still hover under the ambit of hate speech just because that truth hurts the sentiments of some members of society. So even when the aim is not to spread hate but to just discuss and reiterate the historical shreds of evidence and records of a particular culture or religion does it amount to hate speech? This thought process may even go to any extent to suppress even the truth. This is a blind spot in law that still needs to be answered. Speech that triggers or has the potential to incite violence is not healthy in a society but a society with such low temperament or intolerance is unhealthier.

The extent of free speech is to be decided on the basis of what is said to be a reasonable restriction as mentioned under Article 19(2) of the Indian Constitution. The Honourable Supreme Court had also specifically analysed this question in the case of *Kedar Nath Singh v. State of Bihar, 1962*. The court had reached the decision that the reasonability test can be fulfilled if we curtail the scope of application of the provision to the circumstances where any expression we make would lead to the incitement of violence.

CHAPTER FOUR

The Double Standards We Stick To

Nevertheless, when we elaborate on freedom of speech and expression, it is necessary to expand the scope of the analysis and be more inclusive as the integrity of the Indian state can be challenged. When the existence and integrity of the Indian state can be challenged and questioned then why would the legislature enact laws to enforce the protection of religious sentiments? The concept of free speech in India seems to grow in a one-dimensional aspect, as when the question is with regards to free speech, we keep pushing our limits of justice in other aspects but we still stick to blasphemy-related laws. But then, we have Section 295-A of IPC in usage.

Therefore, the point that one keeps pondering about is the convenience in bringing in the issue of free speech when the discussion is about sedition but the vacuum that is created when a question of religious sentiment is involved. The state cannot become less important than religious freedoms as one must not forget that it is through the state that one gets the freedom of speech and expression.

Therefore, if the path we are up to is for absolute and free speech, there has to be equitable treatment across subject matters. This cannot be used as Thus if we are for free speech absolutism, there has to be some sort of uniformity across the country. We cannot abuse free speech as a shield to protect our one-sided bias and give a free pass to the one we approve of.

CHAPTER FIVE

Position of Intermediaries

In April 2015, this judgement was delivered and it was a vital and refreshing starting point to ensure that the fundamental essence of democracy in cyberspace was enshrined and arbitrary prohibitions were not thrust on the depth of free speech and expression. But this was a wonderful platform that the Honourable Apex Court could have utilised to carve a niche and bring out a better-defined position concerning the liability of an intermediary.

This can be understood from how the Honourable Supreme Court addressed the challenges that were present under Section 79(3)(b) of the Information Technology Act, 2000 and Rule 3 of the Intermediary Guidelines, 2011. The analysis of these provisions and regulations was restricted to the last six paragraphs starting from Para 112-118, except from the holding in Para 119(c). The analysis of the main provision was itself curtailed to Para 116 and 117.

In Para 116, the Court took notice of the mechanism that functions under section 79(3)(b), under Section 69 A of the IT Act, it is possible to block the contents of a website

1. By issuing a detailed order through a Designated Officer citing reasons and administering the procedural safeguards as given under the act and the 2009 rules or
2. If it is given by any order of a competent court that directs the designated officer to take any action to block a particular content or website.

Moreover, the Court had clearly emphasised that an intermediary was not expected to decide whether to block content in accordance with Section 69A, in contrast to Section 79(3)(b). This prompted the Court to interpret "actual knowledge" under Section 79(3)(b) to imply receiving a court order ordering the intermediary to promptly remove or prevent access to content.

The Court has clearly stated this in Paragraph 117. In this way, the ruling gave intermediaries some much-needed relief from the conflict between the person who issued the notice and the users they were obligated to serve under the terms of their websites.

What is important to note is that the Court did not explicitly indicate in its analysis that receiving a notification from the appropriate government or its agency would also constitute actual knowledge when defining what "actual knowledge" means. In other words, the Court did not explicitly declare in its reasoning that receipt of a notification from the appropriate government would also constitute actual knowledge, which is important to note when interpreting what constitutes "actual knowledge" in legal cases. At the end of Paragraph 117, in relation to Article 19(2), a reference to government notification is found. Quoted below is the relevant excerpt:

"Also, the Court order and/or the notification by the appropriate Government or its agency must strictly conform to the subject matters laid down in Article 19(2). Unlawful acts beyond what is laid down in Article 19(2) obviously cannot form any part of Section 79. With these two caveats, we refrain from striking down Section 79(3) (b)."

Given below is the excerpt of what the Apex court concluded in Para 119(c):

"(c) Section 79 is valid subject to Section 79(3)(b) being read down to mean that an intermediary upon receiving actual knowledge from a court order or on being notified by the appropriate government or its agency that unlawful acts relatable to Article 19(2) are going to be committed then fails to expeditiously remove or disable access to such material. Similarly, the Information Technology "Intermediary Guidelines" Rules, 2011 are valid subject to Rule 3 sub-rule (4) being read down in the same manner as indicated in the judgment."

Analysis of The Position

The Way Forward

Unanswered is the question of whether such a reading down hinders individual protection because illegal content (that may cause damage or loss) would be accessible to the public until a court order or administrative order is obtained, which may take a long time. Therefore, innocent civilians who have genuinely been defamed online by any intermediary will need to go through a lengthy process before contacting the authorities. The judgement also made it clear that the court's order and/or the appropriate government's or agency's notification must carefully adhere to the topics outlined in Article 19(2) of the Indian Constitution. It goes without saying that Section 79 cannot apply to illegal conduct that goes beyond what is specified in Article 19(2).

The judgement has limited the ability of intermediaries to censor content privately because doing so would require a court order or notification from a government body. Additionally, there are no restrictions on the covert suppression of secretive government takedown requests because they must and should follow the limitations established by Article 19. (2). Indian businesses whose business model is based on the internet are likely to benefit significantly from the judgement to read down the terms of Rule 3(4) of the Intermediary Rules and thereafter apply the benefit of Section 79 of the IT Act to the broad community of Intermediaries. It is further argued that by issuing this judgement, the court effectively terminated an intermediary's duty to do due diligence in India, as intermediaries will no longer be required to exercise due diligence concerning objectionable content on their websites but rather will have to wait for a government notification or order to do so.

CHAPTER EIGHT

Conclusion

The Supreme Court is attempting for the first time to strike a balance between concerns about freedom of expression and the appropriate application of intermediary liability. This is a commendable start considering the complexity of internet intermediary liability.

However, the nature of the Internet necessitates the development of new procedural protections that will provide users access to other, more conventional protections like a hearing and the chance to appeal a wrong decision. Transparency and online notification of blocking is essentially the online equivalent of the written government notices that protect our rights in the physical world. Therefore, in order to keep up with the developments in the digital world, our regulatory framework and our understanding of fair procedure must also change.

www.ingramcontent.com/pod-product-compliance
Lightning Source LLC
Chambersburg PA
CBHW071231140726
47996CB00004B/1564